Snowflakes and Mistletoes

A WINGLESS DREAMER ANTHOLOGY

Edited by
Ruchi Acharya
Kelly Sargent

D1302207

Thank you so much for all your efforts and support that you gave to me in past few months. I'm very happy to receive the book as it is my first time when my poem got published and I want thought to show my gratitude to you through this mail. Hope we get to work together again in the future and wishing you all the best for future endeavours.- Mitali Prasad

I'm literally in tears right now, oh my God. Thanks you @winglessdreamerlit !! The books arrived and are AMAZINGLY FANTASTIC! The cover art is beautiful, the collections stunning! I am filled with such surprise and honor my pieces were published with you, it makes me the happiest lassie in the world. Thank you so much!! If you want to support on of the best publishers EVER, go to Winglessdreamer.com or search their books on Amazon! So grateful. -Gratia Serpento

Hi there, I just wanted to say that after reading some of the poetry on Wingless Dreamer, I feel inspired and in awe. I've been writing on and off as a hobby for a few years now but seeing what you've done and how you've built this whole community of writers, I'm really inspired and impressed. You've given me just a bit more inspiration to keep working on my projects and for that I thank you.- Ryan

Best of afternoons! I am simply sending this email to first thank you for this as I am truly humbled by your decision to accept this poem for publication. I wrote this poem after many nights of night terrors and panic attacks due to my looming anxiety over the pandemic and instant changes the world is going through seemingly overnight. Your validation of this poem is received by such validation and a feeling of triumph that I cannot put into words, so genuinely, thank you. -Arnaldo Batista

I am most excited to receive this new book, and I have already shared your various publications with many friends and family! I am very happy to have come across your publication and look forward to reading many more of your other contributor's pieces!- Natalie Kormos

I shall be anxiously awaiting the book's arrival. I always appreciate your editing efforts. They have always been terrific in the past. More book graphics sounds great, I'm excited to see what they are all about. I'm going to your website now and check out what else you have going on, I know you always have a lot going on. You folks are a great publisher in my book, and I'm not just saying that because you've published some of my work, I sincerely mean it and my family and friends agree. Keep up the great work that you do, I know you will.-William David

Keep up this excellent work. Poetry truly connects the readers with poetic souls across countries and cultures – Amita Sanghvi

It is a great joy for me that a kindhearted editor of a journal like you has liked my poem. Thank you again. Be happy in life this is my heartfelt wishes to you.-Sandip Saha

There is such a positive vibes from Wingless Dreamer, unlike any other publisher. -Gavin Bourke

It's an honor and a privilege to be part of the most eminent Literary Journal of the young minds 'Wingless Dreamer.' This is a place where dreams becomes reality. Wingless Dreamer has made possible for all poets & readers to flap the wings of dreams, imagination & aspiration into the deep blue sky of peace, progress & prosperity. You may prosper like the locket of Apollo. You may win unnumbered hearts of poet lovers in future. – Mr. Saheb SK

Wingless Dreamer

UPLIFTING WRITERS AND ARTISTS THROUGH OUR CREATIVE COMMUNITY

SNOWFLAKES AND MISTLETOES

Edited and compiled by

RUCHI ACHARYA

ABOUT US

In 2019, Indian author Ruchi Acharya dreamed of a literary community that could bridge the gap between fellow, emerging writers with a fervent passion to create and the world of traditional publishing. She envisioned a place where writers and artists are allowed to publish based solely on the merit of their creative skills. Her desire and inspired vision culminated in the design of Wingless Dreamer Publisher, a forum providing aspiring and experienced creators alike the opportunity to share their love of English literature and art on a global platform.

Throughout the year, our Wingless Dreamer team offers a multitude of themed writing contests designed to stimulate fresh ideas and present an opportunity for talented authors worldwide to contribute perspectives through creative expression efforts. We select the best of the best submissions and stream together the components of writing, editing, and illustrating to result in publications of beautiful literary anthologies that we promote in the marketplace. Our commitment to providing this single platform and process allows our authors and artists to bypass challenges and obstacles associated with the traditional publishing goal, and instead maintain their focus and devotion to creating works of art.

Most meaningful is that Wingless Dreamer community members become part of a family, and are guided, encouraged, and supported as they take each step toward cultivating a successful writing or art career. Non-native English-speaking authors are also granted access to free reviews, critiques, marketing, and, in some cases, funding for their work. Our community has slowly, but steadily, grown to become a prominent stage featuring well-known professional writers and artists from all over the world.

Finally, we at Wingless Dreamer are devoted to publishing poetry, fiction, and artwork reflecting the entirety of multiple perspectives and varied experiences extracted from the deep well of soulful human existence. As such, BIPOC, LGBTQ, disabled, minority, and other marginalized voices are especially invited to join in the sharing. Our ultimate goal is to uplift the human spirit through a diverse creative community. At its core, the human spirit desires connections through expressions. We ardently endeavor to gift wings to these heartfelt dreams.

FOUNDER'S PEN

Being a writer can sometimes be solitary and quiet. A writer can understand how it feels to fall in love with every single character, battle with dialogues, work with vivid poetic devices, endeavor for perfection, and build an entire universe from scratch. Guess what? You're not alone. We understand the efforts you put every day into your work. Since we are a team of writers and artists too.

The writing industry is always considered as something obscure and profound by the public in general. It has become so difficult to stand alone and to stick with a writing career in the commercial society we live in today. Compared to other financial and economic-related jobs, things related to writing are the minority.

Writing is a terrific passion, and writers work in a hard industry, one where success is often sought and little received. Writing is not merely something we do, but something we are, and that makes it one of the most challenging of all pursuits in life.

I never got the right support to become a writer at the prime youth of my life. In the place where I come from writing is considered a cute hobby instead of passion - a commitment that writers made to themselves. Writers don't receive the same respect that other professions do. It's quite condescending. That sort of mentality is also so harmful to amateur writers' confidence. From my past experience, I realize that this issue needs to be addressed.

People need to understand that writing is a hard business. It is time-consuming and after dedicating late-night hours, a roller coaster of emotions to finally produce a piece of literary work that might be read around the globe.

So, I come up with this publishing company and yeah I am proud of it.

In the end, I would like to urge all the people who are reading this to never ever give up on your dreams. Seize the day. Every day counts. I hope you will support us and encourage our team efforts. Looking forward to working with you. More power to your pen. Cheers!

-Ruchi Acharya, Wingless Dreamer Founder

JUDGE'S PEN

KELLY SARGENT

Reading Winter poetry reminds us of what sets this time of year apart from the other seasons. Though the earth is entering into hibernation, talented poets have a way of awakening us and our senses to unique pleasures: spotting the first ornate snowflake and glimpsing the mystical winter solstice moon in the sky; warming our hands over the wood stove on a blustery afternoon and listening to comforting crackles from a fireplace aglow; inhaling the aromas of sumptuous holiday feasts and, of course, swallowing that first sip of rich hot chocolate after polishing off a crisp holiday sugar cookie. Wrapped in a fleece blanket and nestled on the sofa, where all you can hear are sounds of sputtering embers and poets' voices in your mind as you take in every vivid image and measured line, holding a mug of steaming cocoa in one hand and a book of poetry in the other truly offers one of winter's most delightful pleasures.

ABOUT HER

Born and adopted in Luxembourg, Kelly Sargent grew up with a deaf twin sister in Europe and the U.S. Her 2021 poetry and artwork, including a current Best of the Net nominee, appeared in dozens of magazines in the U.S. and abroad. She also worked as an American Sign Language interpreter and wrote for a national newspaper for the Deaf. She has acted as a creative nonfiction editor for a literary journal, as well as a reviewer for an organization dedicated to showcasing works by sexual violence survivors.

CONTENTS

🏆 - Grand winner of the contest

🏆 - First runner-up 🏆 - Second runner-up ♉ - Top Finalists

1. THE FAÇADE OF LOVE

Enchanted in the deep forest,
Twinned shadows show destinies path.
Timeless rays shower within,
The wind whispers its forever tune.

Fortunate again that our paths crossed.
The Princess with the mystical eyes,
Is this a dream within a dream?
'I'm from your future past...'

Shadows waver tall with the flame fall,
Fireflies fill the worlds above.
If solitude brings you closer,
would the woods help remember?

Countless times we felt the heavens.
The tunes we sang together,
Distant echoes of a love so true.
The sorrows that we have been through.

If fate casts another path,
If eternal love is what we seek,
Sleep in peace my dear love,
For You are my eternal princess

VASEEM THABREZ

Vassem Thabrez is a passionate person who spends his time touring the forests of Tamil Nadu and works at Apple to fund his conquests. He is a poet, pianist, adventure seeker, gym freak, and food lover. He speaks Tamil, English, and Hindi. Currently, he lives in India with his green buddies. Instagram: rezcraze

2. A WINTER DUSKING

Black-striped white, all palled with blue.
Deep featureless clouds, gray, flake
snow soon splintered by arthritic boughs
bent along scoliotic trunks.

Cold and colder with the closing of the day.
Bluer with each moment come, minute gone.

The blackness of the trees glows darker
with every ray of light that's lost,
spreading like carbon breath from forest lungs.

Night welcomes the world
such as the captor asks of the captive.

One instance, this—rare temporal fleeting:
where killing won't keep the killer breathing.
No, here, survival is solitary:
warmth and if warmth holds.

Heartbeats in the bitter stillness,
hidden, holding their microcosm of warmth
in this cosmos of cold,
left wondering if the memory of morning
is a dream.
A dream to only
be found again
in a dream
in a sleep
in the snow
in the night
where
only time
only might
move.

ERIK DIONNE

Erik Dionne is a musician and high school English teacher living alongside his wife, Jane, in St. Mary's County, Maryland.

3. THE LIGHT WAS LEAVING

The light was leaving
slowly so we would not notice
declining
Slanting every day more acutely
softening
Leaves lifting off
a swirling promenade
to nowhere
The air thin
as your last breaths
Soufflé clouds soft as lungs
exhaling
The sky was Vivaldi's winter
ritornello
All up bowing and pizzicato
the mournful legato of the cello
echoing
never to hear spring again
And you never to return
not even briefly
The angel of Bethesda
no longer stirring the waters
of the house of mercy
Your miracle would not come
You would not pick up your mat
and walk towards me
There would be no more waiting
no lingering goodbye
The sun would set suddenly
dipping beyond the edges
of understanding
And the long dark of night would
spread its epicedium
overtaking us
Surprising us
with a starless end

JENNIFER MARIANI

Jennifer Mariani was born in Zimbabwe. Her work has appeared in Mosi oa Tunya Literary Review, Uproar, Off Topic Publishing and The League of Canadian Poets. She has been a guest poetry judge for Off Topic Publishing's poetry contest. Jennifer resides in Calgary with her daughters where she teaches ballet.

4. ROOTS

At times I need to soft remind
Myself of roots long lost.
The trees I touched that followed through
The clash of iron 'n rust.
Fingerprints across the globe
Did kiss upon my soul
From Celtic hoards to civil wars
Our names along did call.
An arrow each and off we shot
To follow in their steps,
And though we may feel lost at times
Their blood runs through our necks.
No country bound unto am I
And yet they all are mine
In scattered fragments in my heart
My saviour trail line.
So when I hear those whispers bland
I smile, down deep I know
They cannot hurt what they can't see;
I'm free as fresh felled snow.

EVA-MARIE

Eva-Marie is a writer and performer based in London. She initially moved to the UK to pursue acting and has been working in the film and theatre industry for over ten years. Her poetry is deeply romantic and often tragic, sprinkled with self-aware comedy and artistic references. Her work is mainly driven by a sense of Hiraeth that came from a multi-national background and a nature-based childhood contrasted with years of living in the city. This constant search for belonging, whether physical or emotional, is the root of her work.

5. TENNESSEE WINTER

Tennessee Winter
The church bells echo
Across the hills of snow.
Houses dance from
Lights put up for show.
Angels hang from lamps
Lining the icy street.
Trees appear in windows
To give passing eyes a treat.
Children pray for winter break
Until the coming new year,
All while dreaming of gifts,
Toys, and Christmas cheer.
A small town's winter
Is something to hold close,
Where all those around
Are the ones that matter most.
Warm, fresh baked desserts
Fill the air with spice,
Mixing with a cozy fire,
For your senses to entice.
Tennessee's season of cold
Leaves some rigid at the start,
Yet all the comforting perks
Can thaw a frozen heart.

JUSTIN BYRNE

Justin Byrne is an elementary teacher in Middle Tennessee. Justin earned his bachelor's degree in Elementary Education with dual minors of Music and English from Middle Tennessee State University. Justin's work can also be seen in Plants & Poetry, multiple books by Poets' Choice, The Parliament Literary Magazine, multiple books by Wingless Dreamer, The Thing Itself, Shift: A MTSU Write Publication, Arc Magazine, and Brick Street Poetry. Justin can be found on his website byrnepoetry.com.

6. ONE MILE WIDE

If I snug tight my two eyes to make it all come back, block out
        any brilliance, dampen the sound to mold in search for you
on the back of my eyelids, the little veins lead me
        to your face, like a map with many tributaries-

There you are, playing your part with your fingers
        enfolding me as they cross behind your back, wrapping me
in the idea of lemonade sipping on a porch, or some similar sugary
        typecast fable, while we watch the sun move up and down, and up

and down until our bodies ripen sweetly, our tastebuds fray
and gently dry up-

All a canard. Instead, an arctic floor in a half bath, a block
        of ice adrift in a weepy brine pooling on the linoleum, carrying me
out to an imaginary sea with an iceberg captain, sloshed
        in the tub and claiming to be several years sober.

From that angle, floor up, a dirty reflection
        of window-framed lights turn red and green, and green
and yellow until all the cars go home. Forsook without a ride
        and still floating, pursuing the subject of a broken compass

I often conjured the moment the pieced-together porcelain of your smile
began to come unglued, perhaps poorly mended at the break-

Impossible to educe. The smear of the watercolors scattered
        on the ground from your throw of our painting palette
obscures the details of the day the beam across your face broke
        out into a glower. I can't recall

beyond your etching of the skin to feel it, feel something, bleed
        the agony out of you while you dull all the kitchen blades.
Beyond the echo of beads bouncing off teak tiles in slow motion, a necklace
        ripping to remember, the Baccarat cat breaks
into a million pieces as it meets the wall- clawing and screaming,

waking the neighbor. The blue hats of the rule pen
their jotters with permanent ink, take pictures of the broken
   parts. You were gone by then, long and lost. Always lost

and awaiting the recidivism of my reach for you. Eventually
I let you down.

Stanzas of years in between that epoch
   and this, I still stir to the moan of wind twisting and floods flashing
around my ears, to the recurrent cry of a glass cat
   running by, illuminated by bolts of lightning

in my brain. A cacophonous siren interrupts my reverie
   not enough to rouse but life-jacketing me like it helps
armor against the mouth of a jealous tornado- one mile wide
   and pelting my tin top with hail, with spite. Each night

it peels back my scalp, blows open my skull and defaces the painted halls
of my nature, just to get a good look at the chasm
you created and crawled into.

LAURA PECK

Laura Peck is from Kansas City, Missouri, and has an eclectic career background. She holds degrees in Creative Writing, Social Work, and Chemistry, which she received from the University of Missouri in Kansas City, as well a medical degree, which she received from Nova Southeastern University in Florida. She is board certified in general surgery and is currently a traveling surgeon, helping to fill service gaps in rural communities. Her writing is inspired by her work and her life experiences, and she hopes to bring a unique perspective to the literary world.

7. THAWING

Thawing – it awoke and saw
        The winter prison freed it's maw

Mountain air pierced both lungs and will
        Gave birth to renewing imagination
Descending with an intend to kill
        Resurrected from petrification
Of some divine, ardent ice
It paid it's ascension's price

After decades of endurance
        And hunger, the festering disease
It gobbled down all crows and ants
        Crawled further down with ease
Yet needles stung with every breath
Stamina was given by coming death

There lay a beat in the village
        Just beyond the rotten wood
"Yonder there – I come and pillage
        Little things don't taste as good
Eat the guide and slay the priest"
Bells chimed in, announced a feast

And when the lungs will hurt no more
        The snow will turn so foul
And the people hear a horrid roar
        Followed by a shattering howl
Then, just then, they will awake
And know, at once, it is too late

Thawing – it awoke and saw
        To rend and claw and further
                thaw

PATRICK MUCZCZEK

Patrick Muczczek is the author of The Subjugation of Will, To Uncover Worth, and others. He is a student of English literature who engages with and writes speculative and dark romantic fiction. Both visuals and narratives can be found at patrick-muczczek.com.

8. THE CONSTANT CANDLE

The third last house on the third last street,
on the way out of the estate.
A single white candle in the third window,
on the left of the right.
The most yellow, living, breathing,
flame in motion.

A constant candle, ever-bright, ever-white.
Effervescent, burning eternal on its wick,
so natural.
Memories of a church called St Martins,
cold and quiet for carols coming up to Christmas.
Seated on the hard wood in the half-dark and the half-light.
Coming into the light, leaving with it,
retained in both pupils of the eyes.
The candles around the martyr,
bearing stigmata.

The clear flame's silhouette behind the crossed-lead lines,
of the windowpane.
Losing your sense of self and time,
in the depth of the dancing shades of yellow.

Perfectly contrasting, projecting, reflecting,
the cold black sky outside through the glass prism.
Lighting, eternally burning, never extinguishing, brightening.
Never ending, never existed outside,
of the realm of the imagination.

GAVIN BOURKE

Gavin Bourke grew up in the suburb of Tallaght in West Dublin. Married to Annemarie living in County Meath, he holds a B.A. in Humanities from Dublin City University, an M.A. Degree in Modern Drama Studies and a Higher Diploma in Information Studies from University College Dublin. His work broadly covers nature, time, memory, addiction, mental health, human relationships, the inner and outer life, creating meaning and purpose, politics, contemporary and historical social issues, injustice, the human situation, power and its abuse, absurdism, existentialisms, human psychology, cognition, emotion and behaviour, truth and deception, the sociological imagination, illness, socio-economics, disability, inclusivity, human life, selfishness and its consequences as well as urban and rural life, personal autonomy, ethics, commerce, science, grand schemes and the technological life in English and to a lesser extent in the Irish Language. He is widely published internationally.

9. WINTER BREAK

It's finally cold in Texas and Silent Night is playing, somewhere.
I'm propped up in a wicker chair drinking Jäger from a princess cup.
I've misplaced my pipe.
There's no magic tonight, and I'm struggling to understand why that is.
A drug deal is happening by the quarantined swimming pool, and I hear
a child crying.
There's a great expanse of darkness before me, beyond this balcony,
broken up by string lights down the block. They float like pin-point
stars on a solitary sea, still, in a windless night.

Somewhere, a shepherd tends his flock
and Mothers
and Fathers
and Sisters and Aunts and Uncles
huddle and bleat together, sharing warmth under the onyx sky.
I haven't seen a crook in ages.

I'm wandering, balancing, on a mirrored tapestry, draped across space
and time. This lineage extends backwards to eternity but then stops,
here, with me. Everywhere I see myself distorted.

If I closed my eyes
and plugged my ears
and huddled bleating as they do,
maybe I'd glimpse a hallelujah chorus
and it would feel like Christmas.

But I can't.

So, for now, I'm drunk and sugar plum faeries flash their backsides to
truckers on the highway.
Those interstate reindeer, hauling and heaving behind coffee-stained
eyelids.
"Happy Holidays" and "Season's Greetings" to the one honest star I
can see from here – dim and distant, faint and forgettable, like a
kindred spirit in the ether.

May you sleep in a heavenly peace you can call your own.

'Tis the season of giving and the lonely sucker looking for a street-corner fix.
Thankfully, I think the crying stopped.

NICK GILLEY

Nick Gilley is "an Artist, more or less". A modern Renaissance man and "capital 'r' Romantic", Nick is a multi-form artist from the woods of East Texas. He lives in the Austin, Tx area with his partner and muse, Elysia.

10. BIRD BRAIN

the dog and the cats lay,
listless, waiting for the heat
to pass. Even the gray cat acquiesces
to the indoors.
Maybe there is nothing to hunt.
Only the bees move today,
and the flies.

Last week the gray cat brought
feathers from three different birds-
a long black one,
a small, soft, black one,
a mangled gray one.
I wanted so badly to grieve
the birds.
Maybe I preen my own ego.,
scold her for her lack
of need.
but the birds don't love me.

I love their feathers on the wall.
I love what I cannot tame.
there is no room for guilt in her soft belly, no
holding of her rough tongue
wasn't the milk of Hades' mother sweet?
someone,
someone must nurture death.

ZOE MCLAIN

Z Winter is a tired parent and queer writer in the PNW, Their work can be (soon) found in Ethel magazine.

11. AFTER THE D&C

** Dilation and Curettage: a procedure to clear the
uterine lining after a miscarriage or abortion.*

We walked in deep snow,
etching our steps
as in stone

Above us, gray
clouds scraped
an ice blue sky

The park sparkled loudly
with the voice of new-
born snowflake
*

She ran from me through
cold wind, and hid
in the belly of a tree

Reason and doubt flew
like sparrows
after winter chaff

When we came to
a swing set, shivering,
she burst her dam of tears
*

At home, we lay awake
in the guts of the night
wondering *what if*

HUGH FINDLAY

Hugh Findlay's writing and photography have been published in numerous magazines and anthologies, in print and online. He is in the third trimester of life. Instagram & Twitter: @hughmanfindlay

12. COLD BLUE

Cold blue
penetrates my veins
and stops the mindless flow
freezing time unbearably
turning my tears to ice

No choice left but
keep on walking as
distraction or surrender
through the darkness of
February blues

Warming hands with breath
of my heart beating
until I feel and move my fingers
until tears melt into healing
and time goes on at last

I see the blue turning to yellow
and flowers growing
through the snow,
flowers growing
through the snow

ELIZABETH VALERIO

Elizabeth Valerio is a poet raised in Brooklyn, New York and currently living in Atlanta, Georgia. Her experience of walking and observing life in the city inspire her craft.

13. THEY GET YOU WHEN YOU SLEEP

When you were 10
you and two pals paid thirty-five cents each
to see *Invasion of the Body Snatchers*
at the seat-creaking Colony Theater
on a slushy Saturday in October
— more than sixty years later
you've seen that original
and three remarkable remakes
all of them getting in your head under your skin
all of them still spooky
all of them still sparking authentic angst
all of them so eerily elemental
so soul-core-captivating:

stirring sleepy suspicions of those you know
— although they appear the same as always
might not be who you think they are who they say they are
your own mother might not really be your mother
your lover might not really be your lover
sleepy suspicions they just aren't themselves
the most recent remake making the paranoid point
friends family members other familiar figures
— anyone everyone anywhere everywhere —
just might be soul-sucking non-human
bland-as-peas-in-a-pod pod people
and *that* might be for the best — the common good.

Scariest of all?
Scariest of all is you.
You might not be your own true self.
You might not really be ...
who you think you are ...
who you say you are.
You might not really be ... you.

ROBERT EUGENE RUBINO

Robert Eugene Rubino was nominated for a Pushcart Prize in creative nonfiction for "Spinning Shame Into Nostalgia" (Hippocampus, November 2016). He has published prose and poetry in various online and print literary journals, including Elysian Fields Quarterly, The Esthetic Apostle, Raw Art Review, MacQueen's Quinterly, The Write Launch, Cathexis Northwest, High Shelf Press, Gravitas, Forbidden Peak Press and Haunted Waters Press. He's old enough to remember the Cuban Missile Crisis and smart enough to solve the New York Times crossword puzzle on Mondays (other days not so much). He lives in Northern California.

14. PRICKLY PEAR

Fierce will and hunger--
this evidence of struggle
is not beautiful.
Rooted in dry red soil,
buried in snow,
frozen and spined:
you might think of *anger,*
but no energy or time
is wasted on anger, or sorrow.

You might think
the canyon walls have not changed here
for over a hundred thousand years--
and there is not time enough to waste
for one more blossoming?
not enough time for that bright yellow
bird from the first dawn
curving above the mesa rim?
one more flower, one more bee, one more seed,
one more vision of daylight?
There is not enough time?

This is not beautiful?

Inside the house,
a man sits upstairs
and reads,
occasionally looking out
the window
at the passage
of clouds.

BENJAMIN GREEN

Benjamin Green is the author of eleven books including The Sound of Fish Dreaming. At the age of 65 he hopes his new work articulates a mature vision of the world and does so with some integrity. He resides in New Mexico.

15. WHAT DOES SHE KNOW?

what does she know about your bed?
(does she know it's where i slept)
does she know it's the first place we had sex?
does she know i used to hold you under those covers
does she know those covers used to be mine
does she know i gave them to you?
does she know about the poems, the letters you keep next to your bed?
does she know about how I wrote them to you,
about how you refused to give them back?
does she know how we used to cook in that kitchen together?
does she know your deepest darkest secret?
have you managed to say it out loud to anyone but me yet?
does she know
that I gave you the bracelet you wore for three years straight?
what does she know about me?
am I your villain?
I hope she didn't know anything at all in the beginning
that you didn't tell her how you were still with me when you met her
how you threw away three years of us
for a night with her
I like to think no self-respecting person
would comply with that
but I don't know her at all
does she know about your ex fiancé?
does she know about the girl after me, who had the same name?
does she know about my grandma?
how you went to her wake, her funeral,
how you cried like I had never seen you cry like that before
I know you bared your body for this girl in a day
but how long did it/will it
take for you to bare your soul?
does she know about the puppy you got—
and got rid of, because you couldn't handle taking care of something
other than yourself?
does she know how that happened the month before she got pregnant?

does she know about the pregnancy test I took
the week you were with her?
does she know how you were with
her
me
and your last ex
all in the same week?
does she know
how you talk about your mother
this woman who gave her whole life for you?
does she know
how you left the girl before me because you didn't want to be a father
and then left me because you did want to?
how you can never make your mind up on anything in the world?
(i know she has to know now, i know she has seen it)
does she know you may never be able to make it down that aisle?
does she know she will be so much better off
if you can't?

ALEXIS CLARE

Alexis Clare is a eleven-time published author, and thrice self-published through Amazon's Kindle Direct Publishing program, with their poetry books, "The Sun and the Moon", "The Sun, and "The Moon" respectively. They started writing poetry with their father as a young adult, and it has kept them alive until today. They hope their writing can save themself, and save the world at the same time.

16. THE ARCHITECTURE OF ABUSE

in this space, wall to wall
carpeting made of broken glass.
everyone else wears shoes
here, but you are made to go

barefoot. you are
scolded for stepping carefully,
for limping, for wincing, for
bleeding everywhere. when

you suggest the flooring
be replaced, glass bottles
are hurled at you to make
the carpeting plusher.

every night, you sort your blood
from the shards, pour it back
into your veins so as not to be
wasteful. miniscule glass

splinters accumulate in
your bloodstream. each pump
of your heart slices you
internally as slivers slide along

soft tissues. this is okay
because then it feels so
comprehensive to be cut that
your feet stop hurting.

RAE DIAMOND

Rae Diamond is an artist, educator, and nature advocate. They weave language, breath, sound, movement, and things found outside into intricate doorways that lead to vast worlds. Her poems appear in Dovecoat and the Arsonist, and her book, Cantigee, will be published by North Atlantic Books in 2022. raediamond.com

17. INVENTORY

Here is something unforgiven.
Possibly words rushed in the pinnacle
of dispute. Somehow resolved
by sighing or sight of the other
head in hand. How wonderful
to make others feel. How terrible
this contribution to the turning
axis. We blame the blowout
on this; the world, a balancing act
scorned by summer solstice
and sticky sweat which we expel
ourselves from each time we stand
rising from daydream and Adirondack chair.
I don't know everything about the devil
but I think this might be his work; us
leaned back barely believing the sun
is separate from skin. Us, brave
from breaking apart and building
something we think to be a bond.

NATALIE ECKL

Originally from Rochester, NY, Natalie Eckl now lives in Washington, DC where she has recently completed her undergraduate degree in English and creative writing at George Washington University. Her poetry has been accepted by Black Fox Literary Magazine and Five on the Fifth which will both be published in the next few months.

18. NOTES TO A HYPE GIRL ON GETTING HIGH

Crush snort smoke inject me
I lick you from the inside out

My heat swarms in your belly
a beehive bolus, I spread out

hummingbird speed, honey thick
riding vessels, tributaries deliver

me to every cell. Flip pain
non-descript, I don't discriminate

erase everything. Soothe the sting
of your mothers empty wedding seat.

Eight thousand nerve endings
in the clit, numb. Mute the joy

of a nieces' arms thrown out
wide for an embrace, the betrayal

of relief. I tempt with automatic
recall that jumps in every synapse.

Daily sweat breaks out without me,
fetal position with nausea until

you find me again. I will never need
you, though I will stay as long as I can.

LIZ HOLLAND

Liz Holland is an MFA candidate at the University of Baltimore and 2021 nominee for 'Best of the Net'. Her work can be found in Marias at Sampaguitas, The Kraken Spire, Remington Review, Little Patuxent Review, and Broadkill Review. She lives in Baltimore with her fur-son Brax.

19. ANOTHER DREAM

Rummaging through the wreckage of memories past
I dream upon a familiar city-block
Where all is reconstruction by rushing years
Except for street signs and one entryway door—
The entry to where I lived when last I saw
The one whom loving yet even now still hurts,
That killing hurt that hearts are hopeless to kill.

That door opens to that day, the saddest
I have lived except when my mother died.
I learned to love in college from a Fort Wayne boy,
And once become Love's servant Its servant will be.
This lover lost that fatal day's not gone;
Never left a day unthought. Inside
That door is everything inside and out!

The lovers meet going their separate ways
Still plodding on the campus where they met
Intent when passing by each other not
To look each other in the eyes although
Passing close and one must speak and one
Must hear and reply. Embracing obligation!
Yesterday, today, and forever these things are told.

From love to dreaming to poems and purple pages;
From soul to soul to souls a-dozen;God
Is Love! So as a father pitieth his children
May Love have mercy on the wounded servants,
Shackled as they are; show them the way
With dreams and friends that likewise they will endure
Till final immolation in Love's flame.

THOMAS PENN JOHNSON

"Another Dream" is submitted by Thomas Penn Johnson who was born on August 22nd, 1943 in Greensboro, North Carolina. In 1966 he received a B.A. in Classical Studies from then-Concordia Senior College in Fort Wayne, Indiana; in 1968 he received an M.A. in English from UNC-G, and he continued graduate studies in English literature and history at Syracuse and Wake Forest Universities. In 1992 he published a collection of poems entitled "If Rainbows Promise Not in Vain." In 2009 he retired from then-Edison State College in Fort Myers, Florida after serving for 26 years as an instructor of English and humanities.

20. THE MIRROR

I'd recognize eyes like yours anywhere-
vacant, gelid, soulless and dark.
Your presence spews toxins into the air,
I'd recognize eyes like yours anywhere.
It's your grimaced face that I wear,
as I stare into the soul that never held a spark.
I'd recognize eyes like yours anywhere-
vacant, gelid, soulless and dark.

ASACIA HERNANDEZ

Asacia Hernandez is a senior at Stephen F. Austin State University studying Creative Writing. Her first publication will be in SFA's undergraduate literary journal this fall. Originally from Washington State, her goal is to travel the world, and write about it too.

21. WORLD WITHOUT ICE

The memory of Svalbard's ice paradise
lost in Slot Canyons
and recalled in the foggy morning.

"Never turn your back to the sea,"
my mother used to tell me.

Swimming today on the
world without ice
and the diesel engine clatters to life.

The Arctic would have been famous
for its sky blue hue.

But droughts and deluges
mix up ocean water
as much as the wind and tides do.

Farmers feel betrayed by their genetic code
and meltdown-proof nukes love geography.

The last of us survived by clinging to radio antenna
and gauging head injuries
by the treacherous sea.

THALIA PATRINOS

Thalia Patrinos is a science writer by day, fire dancer by night.

22. THOUGHTS BEFORE I DIE

Momma I died today.
I seen it coming,
from the look on his face,
I didn't belong in this place.

Momma he trapped me in.
I couldn't run.
I tried to escape his gun.
Bang!
The bullet pierced my lungs,
the air leaves with each breath,
the blood rushes out,
I knew there was nothing left,
to say,
my life was ending this way.
Momma please don't cry for me,
you did your job as far as I can see,
it was he who failed me,
left me lying for dead,
and now my last thoughts are,
I wish I wouldn't gotten out of my bed.

SHARNTA BULLARD

Sharnta Bullard started writing poetry at a very young age. She published her first poem at age eleven. She currently works as a medical technician in the military, but continues to pursue her passion of writing. Additionally, she also has a master's degree in Human Service Counseling. She is an advocate of helping people find their why and voice. She is currently living overseas.

23. DANCING TOGETHER

Whenever we part,
the songs in an empty sky,
every note dancing
inside a beautiful cage,
like a lyrebird calling out.

A lyrebird calling
for the moon at dawn, its dreams
far past the tree line.
Rounded together, its wings
stretched out against gravity.

Against gravity,
we churn the air with our grief,
live in the future
wreckage of desolate nights.
The lift we seek lives inside,

lives and lifts us, free
of what might happen, lifts us
past forests and floods
when we become this flyer.
The wind takes us where it will,

takes us everywhere
at once, past lakes and ledges,
past this horizon
to the next hearth, everywhere
a fire burning just for us,

a fire pouring out
like water into nothing,
spilling out like milk.
Who nurtures this thirsty flame?
Everything it consumes, ash.

It consumes this grief
when it sings in agony,
notes through the reeds, a night song.
When you left I could not speak
until the coals burned brightest,

until your life burned
the edges of my knowing
how to bury your ashes,
how to carry all this thoughts
of being here, and you not

being anywhere
that I can fathom, any
hand that I could hold
and help across that narrow
bridge you had to cross alone.

To cross an ocean,
the bridge of your little ship
large enough for you
to navigate the heavens.
All you needed were the stars,

the stars and an ear
to hear what others blocked out.
Remember that one song?
You said it embarrassed you,
how easy to transcribe it,

how easy to know
each note in that moment's song,
how free from past and future
worries and ecstasies, free
to sing your one song right now,

your one song right now,
a jar overfilled with light

from a thousand suns,
and the sound of breaking
glass, your life a thousand more,

your life a river
that sustains us, that turns
us into millers,
opening our hearts like grain,
compassion the bread we make,

compassion, the sound
of your voice, a homing sound
we hear in the storm.
Even if we can't see you,
we're moved toward that kindness,

toward the beauty
of the music, all those words
singing together.
What you tried to say says more
when we yield and kiss the ground.

When we yield to love,
what need for escape, what fear
could hold us hostage?
When the sun came up today,
I laughed. Everything opened.

Everything lightened,
my soul circled like a bird
gliding thermals at daybreak.
When I was a child, I flew
in my father's outstretched arms.

And my arms outstretched,
both of us, flying in one
flock, tasting freedom.
What do I need to give now

to become my simplest self,
to become a drink
of water and quench your thirst?
On all that matters,
I give up trying to know
and grieve all that I have lost.

All that I have lost
was first given, accepted,
then fed to the garden.
It fed me and all my friends,
today our celebration,

our celebration
of everything green in us,
what shoots have risen
out of the furrows, the dark
loam of all that worried us.

All that worries us
a frantic squirrel, like a dog
jumps at a maple,
we hoard and scurry, our hearts
as sharp and hard as needles,

sharp and hard as wind
mid-March, the buds in tight fists
against the onslaught.
This spring will find us locked up
inside, watching the branches,
inside like water
collected in clay cisterns,
a long drought ahead.
Inside the mind that seed pod
curled up like lotus blossoms,

curled up like a bowl
that waits for the soup ladle,

the shape that I'm in
before sunrise in this house
before light pours through the pane,

before light swallows
the dark again, a new day
unfurling, oak leaves
as promised in the front yard.
You said, These do not matter.

If we do not breathe
out and seed the world with song,
then what does it matter
if we disappear? What is
the sound of breathing one song?

The sound of breathing
is the only coin I hold—
right now everything
possessing me, the furnace
agrees to share the journey

and the journey asks
for more sun than rain, gets both
to refresh the mind,
the mind and world being one
path over the next mountain.

Up the next mountain,
sedge grass and Saxifraga.
These roots will break stone.
Yesterday in the valley,
the sound of peepers dreaming,

the sound of dreaming
like a green engine humming
throughout the body,
the brace and scold of wind

late-March when the sun goes down.

CHARLES COTE

In 2020, I wrote 5 lines a day, connecting each poem to the day before much like a crown of sonnets. I've submitted the pens I wrote in March at the beginning of the pandemic. I am a clinical social worker in private practice locally, and author of I Play His Red Guitar (Tiger Bark Press, 2019) and Flying for the Window (Finishing Line Press, 2008). I teach poetry at Writers & Books and serve on the boards of 13thirty Cancer Connect, and the Society for Descriptive Psychology.

24. A SECRET VISIT

The way she would say: *I am fine,*
from eyes pink as soft tissue,

sadness like tangles of surf grass,
a constant, if invisible, drizzle.

I wonder now, though of course it's too late,
about a pilgrimage inward with her

—to see little cottages built
for when hints of menace turned ugly.

Gardens she dug— hands deep in the dirt
tending roses red enough to look bloodened—

like those posed with, in her favorite photos
—one arm, a bit showy, stretched out with grace,

her right hand bent slightly back in toward her face,
holding up a beauty for the camera.

I might be privy to tea, even old talks with G-d,
winter foxes in sweet-orange fur repeating "the earth needs you."

There would likely be peace, a refuge for the heart
—*she*, herself, the light that never kept her in dark.

ELLI SAMUELS

Elli Samuels is a poet now living in Texas, having spent many years in the Pacific Northwest. Her latest work is featured or forthcoming in Pif Magazine, Horse Egg Literary, Maudlin House, and an Anthology published by Oregon Poetry Association. She is the author of "Cooking with Elli: A Delicious Guide for Budding Foodies and Beyond" (2014), a yogi, a runner, and is never without passion for a stellar cup of coffee.

25. THE BOY

The barrage of tragedy is too much to bear some days.
The shocking pictures of Americans exercising their 1st amendment rights with violence,
The hundreds of thousands of people dead, the ever increasing hostility.
We have to look away or it will break us.

Then you see something that is too much; one step too far; one horror too many.

I've tried distracting myself.
I've tried understanding and accepting that there is nothing I can do.
I've tried, but that doesn't always work. And it isn't working with the boy.

His name is Arthur Labinjo-Hughes.
He died on June 17, 2020 at the hands of his parents.
His last words were recorded; "no one in the world loves me."

And this is the straw.

This boy..this baby who died alone never knowing one minute of love.
This is my straw.

I'm not even thinking about unloved children and the unfairness of it all.
Maybe then I could volunteer and try to help other children like Aurthur, children in need.
Maybe then I would feel like I am helping in some small way.
Like I'm not powerless.

Instead I can only think of him.

I desperately wish I could have at least been there to hold him.
Not save his life just at least let him know he was loved.
That he was glorious and unique.

A mother's love is fierce and real and I desperately want him to have had that.

If only for a minute.

When the pain and the problems are too much it is natural to reach for help.
To hope there is something bigger that can hold us close and drive away the darkness.
No matter who or how; I find myself in that place.
Nothing left to give; desperate and too afraid to even hope.

So now is when I ask the universe, or God, or karma; please give me this one small thing. Let me be with him when he needs a mother most.

Rearrange the universe in this one small room, in this one small apartment in the vastness of forever. Rearrange just a few seconds so he doesn't have to die alone. Give me the chance to take him away as the people who should love him most beat the life from him.

Let me hold him tight so he knows he is loved.
Let the last words he hears be mine.
Let me tell him he is loved.

That he was loved.

KELLEY DOLSON

Kelley Dolson is a retired, bipolar Navy veteran who lives with her son and two cats in rural Oregon.

26. BEING ALIVE OR BEING EXHAUSTED?

Been feeling like it's the end for me.
Cannot breathe anymore of this dirt in my head
Cannot taste anymore of this sourness that i feel my life has become
Everything seems fine, yes.
But it is not good enough for me
I feel like running away
And I don't want a stop
I just want to keep running
Until my legs break apart
And the white bones in my spine become blood red
and I want to run blind
The scenery fills no purpose in my life
I do not need to see faces or nature or any of that bullshit
I just want the speed to takeover
I'm more used to being hurt than anything
So it's okay
It's my comfort zone
And I don't think that's sad
I just think it's painfully honest
Living becomes harder every hour
The harder it gets, the less blood I feel in my body
My veins dry up like a dessert.
Honestly, I think I am just exhausted
That's normal right?
Being exhausted every second, every day
With everything and nothing at the same damn time
I wake up, I do not want to
My mind says try, and my body says 'shut up'
My mind says 'please, try?' And my body says ' I said shut up' How
am I to live like this?
How am I to breathe?
How am I to stay calm in this world of extreme chaos?
Should I just give up? Let it go?
I know all of this is in my head
I wish I could tear apart my brain into pieces
Keep the disturbed pieces away from the okay ones

And I try to fix the disturbance piece by piece
Life then would become easier I think.
It would become bearable I think
To know what works and what doesn't
I can throw the wrong ones out you know?
And then, only then my brain would be a better place to live in.

SHREYA TOMAR

Shreya Tomar is a sophomore at New York University, majoring in Psychology and minoring in Child and Adolescent Mental health studies. She is a passionate writer and has always tried to understand her own feelings by writing them down into words and stories. Her passion for poetry began when she was 15 years old with her first love. Since then, life has been like a rollercoaster ride for her but she chooses never to give up.

27. THE HEART CRAWLS BACK HOME

...the door icebound
this steel-built morning.

Right broken arm of the blue fir,
hesitant diver, flirts with the ground.

A shattering, should it fall.

Lying atop stoic brown boxwoods
not the brutalized limb flung wide in a storm

but a grackle.

This one a river bird netted with heaven's spittle...
late winter's lacquer

      ...epoxy of furor.
fixed.

What misconception of courtship has brought it
to this mountainside cabin?

What navigational failure
has left it here for too long?

What witness would dwell in
so fractured a landscape?

Cruel purposeless solstice
remote in its silence, it sends heart away,

numb.

ROBIN WEISER

Robin has returned to her city roots after living in New York's Shawangunk Mountain Ridge for many years. She is a returning student and writer of poetry, and is very, very happy not to have to carry firewood or clear snow any longer.

28. THE SWARM

A small tornado of wing-ed death peckers
And the *ohs* and the *ahs* of my daughter...

Dear
  invisible
corpse

where you may lie is beyond my reach,
beyond my sense of smell,
too far from the crowded huddle of corpses

that we will become.

Yours is a place in a field

                  or by a wood

                                  soft and

dark

Somewhere in the shallow grasses of a nigh winter's edge
there,
      by the parched plain,

you're curled into yourself,
the last vestige of a prenatal spawn.

How you died!

before you were born, the warmth
you must have felt—

Your mother ate the clover of life,
chewing the cud of satisfaction;

she gave you a chill when you were birthed
and anointed you with her tongue, as you cried
and snuggled your way to her breast,

but the terrible implementation of time gives way
to a fetal death curl

there, where the great   black

    birds

of corruption swarm to a frenzy.

DR. KHALIL ELAYAN

Dr. Khalil Elayan is a Senior Lecturer of English at Kennesaw State University, teaching mostly World and African American Literature. His other interests include finishing his book on heroes and spending time in nature on his farm in north Georgia. Khalil's poems have been published in A Gathering of the Tribes magazine, Dime Show Review, About Place Journal, and The Esthetic Apostle. Khalil has also published creative nonfiction, with his most recent essay appearing in Talking Writing.

29. ADVENT

winter's early here
its teeth bite me with an unrelenting fury
scoring my bones with a universal sadness

there's no holly in my halls
only shadows of everything
taken by the tide and the mocking smile of time

there will be more punishment to come
quartz snow blanketing the future
with a sardonic smirk

leathery skin cracking open
bleeding the sand of regret on the icy driveway
cheeks embellished with salted diamonds

i go in search of a shovel
to clear a path
to the unknown

RC DEWINTER

RC deWinter's poetry is widely anthologized, notably in New York City Haiku (Universe/NY Times, 2/2017), New Contexts 2 (Coverstory Books, 9/2021) Now We Heal: An Anthology of Hope, (Wellworth Publishing, 12/2020) in print in 2River, Event Magazine, Gargoyle Magazine, Genre Urban Arts, Meat For Tea: The Valley Review, the minnesota review, Night Picnic Journal, Plainsongs, Prairie Schooner, San Antonio Review, The Ogham Stone, Southword, Twelve Mile Review, Yellow Arrow Journal, The York Literary Review among others and appears in numerous online literary journals. She's also a one of winners of the 2021 Connecticut Shakespeare Festival Sonnet Contest, anthology publication forthcoming.

30. MOON'S MISTAKE

It was December 19, 1985
We must've been seven, right?
You had never been in a courtyard more frozen in your life—
the grass, pines, your fingertips swimming in wool
Peoples' voices pounding in stampedes
Snowflakes growled like engines

Your town in shambles from a leaky moon
It's all my fault
I didn't ask for help
At least, not from the alchemists
And now everything is ruined for you

I tried too hard
I didn't try enough
I didn't listen enough
I should've stopped moving so fast
Talking
Now it's cold, empty, and without the smell of licorice--
Total ice

She, the moon was furious
Your town,
A wreck

The moon--
She knows you will die thirty-four years later
She knows the Earth will slice you into artful shards
Your strums will die
Whiskey-soaked
Alone, near your desk

I couldn't stop it
Because the moon was overcome
by the masculine that year
Bleeding out in violet-purple clots

Moon dwelled deep in quartz stone
Rose, transparent, love in the iris of her galactic eyes
Her tears streaked the sunrise
And you couldn't move—
Frozen
Knowing you'd be dead in thirty-four years

ELAINA BATTISTA-PARSONS

Elaina Battista-Parsons is a writer across genres. She also works as a reading coach for students with disabilities. Elaina loves ice cream, antiques, pop culture, and snow. Elaina's poems and essays have been published by Backlash Press, Burnt Pine Magazine, Vine Leaves Press, Spring City, 3Moon Magazine, and Read Furiously. She also has an upcoming YA with Inked in Gray Press in Fall 2022 and a vignette collection with Vine Leaves Press scheduled for 2/22 release.

31. BELOVED MOTHER

Dear beloved mother, I hope you're doing well
gulping that third martini in a hotel room in Hell.
Frankly it's a miracle that I have survived
so pardon me if I don't care when or where you died.

Nightmares of you and grandma soaking up the booze,
two drunks under one roof, children gonna lose:
I grew up too fast, my sister couldn't cope,
I became a robot, she just gave up hope.

When I was a young boy, you said I was too fat;
how is a 10-year old supposed to deal with that?
Became obsessed with working out, took it to the extreme
but what good is it to be ripped if you still lack self-esteem?

The martinet that was you, obsessed with etiquette,
put books under our armpits, like soldiers we would sit—
Not even God could save us if a book fell to the floor:
A hard slap to the cheekbone, boorish manners underscored.

If we weren't hungry or couldn't finish a meal,
that was the beginning of another abusive ordeal:
The food stayed on the table until we'd finally eat
even if after three days there was mold on the meat.

At church on Sunday mornings we played out a charade
holding hands and smiling, marching as on parade.
Of her well-dressed family perfect mother was so proud
while we inside were dying but couldn't cry out loud.

Even at nighttime cringing in our beds
there were no dreams of unicorns drifting through our heads:
Here came beloved mother brandishing her belt;
before school every morning— make-up on every welt.

My loving little sister could never break free

shackled as she was to the family tree:
Father old and absent after the divorce,
I was off at school—things would only get worse.

After school she'd find you passed out on your bed
and have to wipe the vomit splattered on your head
but it wasn't very long until sister heeded your call
and she went you one better—drugs PLUS alcohol.

As I become an old man, only now I realize
how much we were cursed emerging from your thighs.
Your deviant behavior had alcohol as its source
but not once in 20 years did you ever express remorse.
You built a wall around your heart, anaesthetized your brain;
You really didn't give a damn about your children's pain.
I've never been a drinker; I saw what my sister went through
but despite a lifelong effort I still ended up like you:
My mind is always racing, I don't want time to feel,
it's safer to be robotic so all emotion I conceal.
I understand the dynamic and that I'm not to blame
but having failed to overcome I'll always be ashamed.
We're taught to show compassion, over this I agonize,
I forgive but can't forget how you ruined your children's lives

and it's you beloved mother whom I'll always despise

WALTER SHULITS

Walter Shulits is an endurance athlete who graduated from the United States Military Academy at West Point. After a lucrative career in creating and marketing bond investments for international pension funds, banks, and insurance companies in North America, Europe, Asia and Australia, he's retired to Provence, France, with wife Catherine but spends up to six months a year in beloved Hawaii.

32. OF FROZEN FIELDS AND SCANTY SEEDS

When bloomy bells and balmy days forsake
A sphere of solstice worn, miasmal skies
Enfold a leaden shroud of winter wake
As falling crystalline array belies.

The oaks are weaned from reach of red and gold,
And held by stranded lines of bleary wings,
With sculptured trunk for base of bastions holed
To brave the brink that famished lustre brings.

From fleeting streaks of gleam, to chartless height
Of icy dunes, now flanked by sleety sheets.
Yet swallowed beds patrolled by frost and flight
Become graves when homing light depletes

For daunting dawns, in lieu of morning song,
Are tempered trills of fretful flits that leads
To lurid storm, with swooping strikes along
A shattered fray from view of scanty seeds.

The roots are rung by spans of wild cascade,
With turning tails as tolls from layers thinned,
When clouds are sated on a tainted glade
And dusky tinge, as lesions stain the wind

Though sunlit lances lift the sullen screen
To galvanise the lines of faded earth
And breach the unthawed walls for vital green,
There are no quills to greet the spring's rebirth.

DANIEL MORESCHI

Daniel is a poet from Neath, South Wales, UK. After life was turned upside down by his ongoing battle with severe M.E., he rediscovered his passion for poetry that had been dormant since his teenage years. Writing has served as a distraction from his struggles ever since. Daniel has been acclaimed by various poetry competitions, including The Oliver Goldsmith Literature Festival, the Westmoreland Arts & Heritage Festival, and the Jurica-Suchy Nature Museum's Nature Poetry Contest.

33. THE MAN IN THE DOOR

You may not believe me,
but I see him there.
The man in the door.
Old layers of porcelain cream flaked away, silhouetting
his ambiguous form.
He is framed between the panels,
a rugged profile as he looks left.
A slight bouffant above his brow,
cascading into a luscious mane that is
cropped behind his head, above his shoulders. A large-bridge nose,
almost bulbous, protrudes over the tiny, chipped mouth
and jagged mountainous chin.

I giggled at his appearance,
(At first)
and nodded hello.
"I shall call you Mr. Timbers,"
I crooned, gently caressing his creases.

Mr. Timbers didn't speak, (Not then)
so I didn't think much of him until I laid in bed, the blankets bundled
around me.
The real live burrito babe.

"Good evening," he grizzled,
"I believe you christened me, Mr. Timbers."

"Oh," I tittered nervously
who was I to name him?
"I do hope that's alright," I sheepishly pursed my lips
and curled my toes tucked deep beneath the blankets.

"Why certainly, its so very charming," he retorted, the knots in his
voice knocking around my brain.

I smiled in flattery, "I must say, I better be off to sleep now."

"Shall I sing you a ditty?" he asked, optimism dripping from his tone.

My eyes grew heavy, as the husky words lulled inside my head.
"Pretty Precious, go to sleep,
visit those splendid dreams,
Pretty Precious, close those eyes,
Listen to Mr. Timbers."

I awoke the next morn
as sunlight burrowed beneath my eyelids.
"Mr. Timbers?" I called, the cry catching in my throat.
Silence returned my call, and my glee fell
hollow into my stomach.

My day dragged, sadly serene, in his absence.
Until that night, as I rested
(Restlessly)
and again, heard his ragged voice tootling into my brain.

"Good evening, Pretty Precious."

"Mr. Timbers!" My cry erupted eagerly.

He sang to me again, raspy pleasantries pooling
deep inside. Our routine now cemented
like the sidewalk pressed
to silty stones.

He came to me
(His voice)
six nights. Always
warbling that melody.

On the seventh night,
I waited, listening
for my tune. Hidden
under the heavy bedspread.

The shadow seeped from the door,
sweeping across the floor and stopping
at my beside. My breath caught,
captured by fright. But then
the shadow formed into a man
(The shape)
and I asked, "Mr. Timbers?"

The scraggly voice
(I'd come to love)
resonated from the dark figure, and he
flowed onto my bed, pressing
an inky palm upon my forehead.
It was burning, a too-hot stone scalding
my skin. But he sang,
and I slept.

He visited
(His shadow)
six nights. Replayed,
over and over, each performance more ragged.
A video tape rewound too many times.

The seventh night,
I crawled under the covers,
ready for the searing touch and crackly speech.

His shadow crept from the door
and traveled to the end of my bed.
He changed then
(Transforming)
quite quickly. The black air hardening
into human. His features defining
before me.

Milky skin,
Black, bushy, hair brushing his shoulders,

and the large-bridge nose
(So round)
stretching outward so impossibly.
Several spikes jutted from his chin
and he grinned, a mouth brimming
with too many tiny teeth.

I gazed into eyes.
Two black marbles pushed
deep into his skull.

He answered me
(Before I spoke)

"Why Pretty Precious,
don't you recognize me?"

And I smiled
(Weakly)
and he sang to me
six nights.

He didn't come to me
(Tonight)
as I set off to slumber.
Frosty gusts
whispering at my window.

I stood and strode
to the hallway, where he stood,
watching the white swept rooftops
and bare splintery branches.

"Pretty Precious," he cooed
(Croakily)
turning towards me.

His twisted fingers
curled around a smooth silver sheen.
The gift extended to me,
its sharp tip piercing his pallid palm.

His other hand pointing a wiry
crooked finger out the window.
"Listen to Mr. Timbers."

ASHLEY EDENS

Ashley is a married mother of 2, who stays home with her children and her pets. She has loved writing creatively for as long as she can remember, and relishes the quiet time during pre-school when she has time to hone her craft. She enjoys writing quirky and eerie poetry and short stories.

34. LIGHTHOUSE TO FREEDOM

I don't know when you crept in,
but I do remember recognizing you that December night
when a bitter nip drilled itself into my bones
In the
> h u s h e d

> > silence of the bare walls within,
I listened to the sound of rain persistently pelting the ground outside,
punctuated by lurid lightning and threatening thunder.
It was then
> that I heard a knock followed

> > > by a *whisper*,
and then again, except this time,
> I *felt* them too.

That hammering came from the hellish black hole **you created**
My insides, usurped and emptied out
so that **you** could build your home.
I felt the whisper trapped in the aching lump within my throat.
Your deadening eyes,
> stealthily

> > > pierced through my
> > clavicle,
regurgitating memories of all those times when
you *beat* my voice into submission.
in the merciless inferno you wielded
My nefelibata spirit was **singed** and **sullied**
down to
> black
> > carbon flakes

> *Dear anxiety,*
You corrupted my narrative with an agonizing exposé that I felt too
> I n a d e q u a t e

> > > to lay out to the world.
You stayed.
You avalanched over all my defenses
as hailstones clattering over fragile walls
You tore through my lungs and left me *gasping*.
You **conjured** storms,
> *cursed* clouds
> > and *cold* winds.

Your growls invaded my ears
And *extinguished* my frenzied crescendo of cries.

In your lightning strike attack, I shrank
to a mere anatomy of
      s-e-v-e-r-e-d dreams and
                          shadowe
                      d fractures,

I almost surrendered my existence to your fire
then realized,
That tongues glazed with lies,
Eventually have their metallic sting rinsed
in pools of ice.
So, In my own capsized condition
I vowed to rebuild myself from flotsam.
I contained your *pouring wrath*
Within my loving vessel.
I understood that while you were burning me,
           you were burning too.
Should you stay, I won't wrestle your rage but
I won't float fracas as I once did.
Instead,
      I have chosen co-existence,
 dear anxiety.
One in which, we can both embrace silence
as we watch sulfurous ash levigate
from the last sienna cinders
yielding slowly from the parts of us that burned.

STUTI SINHA

Stuti is an Indian writer from Dubai. She writes about the human condition and emotions in poetry and prose. She is also an avid musician and passionate about discovering cultures and human experience through travel. She currently has no publication history

35. A FLOWER THAT BLOOMS

A flower that blooms
Blossoming in its graceful splendour on the dawn of a new day
The first touch of light
coruscating through.
Seamlessly flowing through a subtle passage of time.
My eyes are drawn to the dazzling and glowing effulgence which
appears out of nothing.... like a sudden burst of energy; a fantasy
shrouded in doubt.

The flower withers, languishing in the cold light of day.
Each petal droops, feeble and weary.
Peeling back the layers of time that once stood still.
Feelings run deep, enmeshed in solitude under the guise of friendship.
Torn things can be fixed, but the change is often harder than the period
of growth.
The key to change is understanding its impermanence.

The flower withers more.

The bee lolling around on a bed of wildflowers.
Below it, stands the remnants of a beautiful flower.
The wildflower with its tall barbed point, detaching from a space it
once inhabited, tethered to its past.
As she spoke, the memory she described was accompanied by a white
plume of breath.

The flower withers once more.

VASAVI KOKA

Vasavi Koka is an Art Educator and a writer. After studying her BA in Art with English Literature and her Masters in Art, Design and Visual Culture she went on to complete her Postgraduate Certificate in Secondary Art Education at The University of Cambridge. Vasavi has since embarked on a successful teaching career and during this time has discovered the importance of creative writing, both as a creative and cathartic outlet. She has recently published her first therapeutic children's book entitled, 'Kokan and Zoya'. As a practising artist and writer She closely observes, and takes motivation from, the visual world around her. In her writing she endeavours to compile exciting poetry and stories which will stimulate the reader or viewers thinking processes, and also open their minds to a world of creativity, multiple perspectives and evocative metaphors.

36. A PROVERB

A woman whose skin is porcelain scribbles FRAGILE on her forehead in red sharpie. Sometimes she wonders if she's alive. Sometimes she lies down on anthills between sidewalk cracks and allows worker-ants to swarm her, hoping they'll find something sweet. Sometimes she has phone sex with a stranger half a world away and imagines the hot breathless voice to fit the lips of a sinless saint in an alabaster body. Sometimes a bathroom mirror lies and tells her she's beauty. Sometimes she disappears into the woods for years and returns with hyssop blossoming purple from her armpits and mourning doves perched on her shoulders. Sometimes she ties her hands behind her back and waits in a midnight parking lot for someone to kidnap her. Sometimes she goes to dinner with men, and she does not eat anything, and her lips do not move. The woman whose skin is porcelain rewrites a proverb from her favorite book again and again on the unpainted plaster walls of her bedroom: no one is anything.

LUCAS CLARK

Lucas Clark writes about his dreams often. He has a reoccurring nightmare where he is chased by black-haired dogs. He doesn't know what this means.

37. I AM LIVING, I AM NOT

I am living, I am not,
I am here and gone;
I am lying on the bed
And I have disappeared;
I am somewhere else instead,
Beyond your outstretched arms.

I am darkness, I am light,
I am lost in the winding sheet;
I am the echo of my steps;
I am the color of my eyes;
I am the song I used to sing
While walking through the door.

WALTER WEINSCHENK

Walter Weinschenk is an attorney, writer and musician. Until a few years ago, he wrote short stories exclusively but now divides his time equally between poetry and prose. Walter's writing has appeared in a number of literary publications including the Carolina Quarterly, Lunch Ticket, Cathexis Northwest Press, The Closed Eye Open, The Writing Disorder, Beyond Words, Griffel, The Write Launch, The Raven Review, The Raw Art Review and others. His work is due to appear in forthcoming issues of the Iris Literary Journal, Pioneertown and Fauxmoir. Walter lives in a suburb just outside Washington, D. C.'

38. SNOW: A DEFINITION

Snow. Noun. Symmetrical architecture.

Six-fold. Always six-fold, each
flake its own crystal palace.

Its weight dependent on place.
In the Eastern US, it's called heart attack snow,
the shovel so difficult to lift. Feather-light
becoming unbearable heavy all together.

Snow settles. Insulates.

Buried deep, things stay warmer.

Snow. Verb. Informal usage. To misinform
or embellish. Example: *The company really snowed
doctors, patients, and the public by minimizing
the medication's danger.*

Each snowflake begins with a seed,
kernel of dust. It only grows by falling.

CARRIE VESTAL GILMAN

Carrie Vestal Gilman lives, works, and writes in Denver, Colorado. She has been a social worker in the medical field for over 20 years. Her prior poetic work has been published in four and twenty, Intima: A Journal of Narrative Medicine, The Human Touch, and in the 2021 Anthology "Stories that Need to Be Told" by Tulip Tree Publishing. She is currently in training to become a certified poetry therapist.

39. FROM GOD

I have left you in a spindrift
Vacuums make no sound
Shout and scream and
Shine your lights and
Send your tin cans into
The Nothing all you want.

If you knew tomorrow,
Woke up KNOWING
that what you have
Is all you get...

Would you change your life?

Who told you to keep time
And build towers and
Totems to yourselves?

Who whispered it was the way
To conquer and conquest
And request it all be served
On a tray of righteousness?

Why did you not follow the example
I left with Her and her creatures?
Be born, live in the moment
And Die
not knowing anything
But the moment and rolling in it

What did I know about politics
Or churches on Rocks?

You were the architects of your plot
Your story unfolded and you told it
Again and again

To impress and depress

But your marble still spins
And your signs unfold
And you still do not behold
Your ice melting
And your oceans belting
Out storm after storm...

After Storm.

What does it take?
You are the architects of your conclusion.

All I can do is watch and pray.

TERRY LAVALLEE

Terry LaVallee is a grade 6 language arts and Maths teacher, 25 years into the profession.
He has dabbled with writing, both pre- and during his professional life, enjoying short fiction
and poetry as his genres of choice. He's a strong advocate for and supports the writing and
voices of youth.

40. FOR ME

These words, they are not for you.
No matter their fit or feel.
Whether they burn or lie frozen through
these words I know are real.

If beyond body lies the soul
then beyond soul lies the pen.
When death lands its final blow
should paper not meet pen, what then?

Read them if you desire
ignore them if you are too wise.
Find them plain or uninspired
it matters not your dangled prize.

Only your own will be enough
if to yourself you remain ever true.
When others find your work too rough
say only, these words are not for you.

JORDAN BRIGGS

Jordan Briggs is an entrepreneur and attorney. His left brain gets to have all of the fun, so occasionally he writes so that his right brain does not melt and seep out of his ear.

41. THE PATH

I've walked on a path of abuse, poor choices, and self-sabotage,
I have no one to blame for the path I find myself wandering on.
The path is embedded into the Earth; it's made of jagged stone, and I am barefoot.
The rocks make cuts on my naked feet.
My feet hurt! It's not enough to cripple, but enough to make me cry.
I push forward, leaving a trail of fire engine blood.
I see relief...there is life-giving water seeping through the stones.
The water cleans my wounds... but I stay too long, and my feet become prunes.
I limp down the rocky path, and the stones eventually turn into planks of wood.
There is no end in sight... all I see is twist and turns.
My tender soulless feet start to get splinters that infest my feet.
The pain becomes too much; I drop to my knees and start to crawl; my knees can take it.
Ultimately, the path turns in cement, my knees start crushing the pavement.
The unforgiving concrete chips away at my bones.
I grit my teeth. The taste of enamel hits my tongue.
The pain becomes too great... I can't crawl anymore!
I'm face to face with the cement. Inch by inch, my belly scrapes the concrete.
Like a human snail, I slog onward.
The path transforms into ice. I'm so cold... it feels like fire against my skin.
I shiver...my broken teeth rattle, body numb, heart frozen, and fingers are frostbitten.
What I wouldn't give for Jack London to make me a roaring campfire to thaw me out.
I slide forward... I feel like I'm almost dead.
Finally, the path ends, I find myself in a field of Kentucky Bluegrass.
The soft Earth feels like a memory foam mattress.
Happiness comes over me like an ocean wave.
A gust of wind fills my nostrils with the scent of lavender.
My body stops hurting, and I gaze at the beautiful grass.

How many people have traveled down the path I was on?
I grip the Earth in my hand and see fragments of bone in the dirt.
I'm surrounded by death. Everyone who finished the path their body fertilized the lush grass.
This is the end of the journey; I let the sun warm my face as I stare at the great blue sky.
I feel my body connecting with the Earth.
I take my last breath...My body is depleted of life.
My flesh becomes part of the Earth, and my spirit ascends into the wild blue yonder.

STEVEN DEE KISH

Steven Dee Kish is a writer who lives in Las Vegas, Nevada. He has endured childhood trauma, and is a survivor of suicide. His writing shows what life is like, when someone is living on the edge of madness/sorrow. The poet is always trying to describe what cannot be said. When Steve shared his writing with the public, it was received with positivity and people confirming that they too hurt, but were unwilling to "put themselves out there", but people found comfort that he was hurting, just like them. Steven's poems have been published in, on-line journals: Continue the Voice (Issue 7 & 8, UK). The Elevation Review (Issue 5, USA), and The Rainbow Poems Review (Issue 4, UK). Steven's poems have been printed in Pure Slush Books (Lifespan Vol 3 & 4 AU). Night Picnic (Volume 4 issue 3). Wingless Dreamer Anthology (Dawn of the day and Book in black).

42. I WAS TOLD TO WAIT

I was told to wait.
She didn't say how I was to wait.
Tonight, there will be no lingerie and no make-up.
I will not submit to being tied with scarves or secured with hand-cuffs.
No toys, no oils, no creams, and no scents.
Tonight, when she gets home, I will be waiting.
She will find me as fresh as the flowers in the vase.
She will see my smile the smile she saw the day we met.
I will tell her nothing with my voice.
However, my body language will speak volumes. I am well rested.
I am eager.
I am willing.
Most of all, I am waiting.
She will weigh the consequences of her actions and determine if the
balance sheet teeters to the
black or the red.
I will lick my lips in a motion barely perceptible to garner a favorable
outcome.
Her hands descend to her skirt hem independent of any cerebral orders.
For her, this is a debate.
For me, this is a forgone conclusion.
Once she takes that penultimate step, I am hers.
Once she takes the final step, she is mine.
Her clothing cascade is gravitationally assisted.
Her pace is proportional to her pulse.
She accelerates.
And yet, I will wait.
As if in a time dilated manner, I can witness each of her refined moves
toward me.
I match each of her actions with my own reaction.
She is mobile.
I am acoustic.
My audible coo reaches her at a precise moment.
She is forever mine.
Some things are worth the wait.

ANDY BETZ

Andy Betz has tutored and taught in excess of 40 years. He lives in 1974, and has been married for 29 years. His works are found everywhere a search engine operates.

43. LOOKS

I am back in my favorite prison
Three drinks and you reveal yourself again
Standing in front of me like a proud nudist
You're as real as the customer in line at the post office
Hurrying to mail a final letter, and I the clerk
Stamping it and placing it in the depository,
You stand out from all, an individual,
A stranger in all accounts but I know you:
You bite your nails like you need a cigarette
Yet you are smoke and smell like it.
Such dim, eager pleasures in life.
Nearly twenty years you've been free
Of that chained body you forced yourself out
You were right in all directions: there are
No coincidences, no chance.
Deep down we yearn to know what's inside us
Praying and clawing at brain and skull;
What it is that walks our feet, how the eye
Sees and that tick of the uncontrolled heart.
But escapees are caught and sentenced
To another body without notice:
No one comes back to this with a story
That would blow the lid on the microscope
And cross charade.
You were that one exception.
With memory, and graveside
Flowers we think the dead hear us
But they're right there right there.
And look: we waste such precious time
walking dogs, eating burgers, on exercise and cartoons.

AUSTIN FARBER

Austin Farber is a writer and photographer from Rose Hill, Kansas. Austin is a Wichita State University alumnus where he studied English literature and writing. Austin's writing and photography encompass different perspectives of people, time, and space. These poems embrace a multilayered combination of mysticism and duality, in an altered state of consciousness. Austin currently resides in Utah.

44. BEETHOVEN'S NINTH

hospitals are orchestras.

beeps and whistles
measure sound.
cardiac arrhythmia
becomes meter.

no,   there are no
encores for this symphony.

pity, pity — too late, the deafening monitor
reaches crescendo —
A FORTISSIMO FLATLINE

as conductor

thrashes.
this movement dies.

after one last bow,
another takes its place.

LEO SMITH

Leo Smith is a graduate student at Spalding University. He prefers the pen to the sword, even
if it less fun to swing around.

45. SONNET: AFTER HOURS

We move from the tangerine light to the dusty corridors of the background.
Sit to mark where we last will be seen before inhaling pounds of fries.
Four in a three seater, ankles on knees, everyone still safely strapped down,
Afraid to move. Not too familiar yet, we breathe in each other's mango
highs.

One of us mutters something about death being so close to us,
like it squeezed into the back, followed us from the beach.
Tarot cards burn through a backpack like they are cursed, but *that's nuts-*
another one of us blurts out. His black eyes turn a malignant peach as he
speaks.

Blank expressions cover the two door space, other drivers even stay away -
as if Emily Dickinson was right, it was like death came in a Honda. But
none of us got in. We stay glued to seats, we all talk to each other like dogs
- *stay.*
 Flip the conversation on its head, we talk about marriage, and how we all
manage

the feelings that come with being exhausted from this place.
We leave the car with nothing but a faint citrus trace.

SYDNEY SHAFFER

Sydney Shaffer is a poet with a degree in creative writing from SUNY Purchase college. She
loves to write detail heavy poetry that ties magical images with realistic concepts. In her free
time, Sydney enjoys going for long walks in the snow, playing with her cat, drinking a hot
cup of coffee, and listening to Taylor Swift's entire discography.

46. HOMELESS HEARTLAND 1913

Your temperature is zero
and the windchill is thirty below.
Oh, Nebraska,
where did your heart go,
beneath grim grimy gray ice and snow?

White billowing drifts in the night,
dingy dark not long after dawn,
truck, bus, diesel soot black,
before a body's homeward bound.

Oh, Nebraska,
where did your big red smile go,
beneath cruel grimy gray indifferent snow?

I saw your gaunt woman.
I saw her kids.
She sold her last in a pen;
two-by-fours, chicken wire, thin.
She needed to eat.
Her children Had to eat
before lone going, long, so far,
in that cruel biting smiling, savage blast of beast.

Oh, Nebraska,
where did your poor children go,
beneath Easter Sunday's ice and snow?
Such cold makes burning, painful leaden marrow.
Such cold hearts rake, harass, and harrow
until that dreaded open-eyed sleep
in road salt, black ice, and howling sleet
keep it secret until a thaw
let a newspaper tell it all.

Oh, Nebraska,
where did your heart go,

with mothers and children beneath the snow?

STUART FORREST

I was born in Omaha, Nebraska in 1951. I took writing courses at Stanford University Continuing Studies and began writing poetry in 2012.

47. FROSTBITE

midnight snow
frosted on
the bottled rain
of the past

weighing heavy within
the darkened chambers
of my heart.

bathing in Northern Lights
every chill remains within
a skeleton
sugar-coated

your
crystalline ice flowers

wither
with every flake

KATE MACALISTER

Writer, Social Justice Witch, and medical student Kate MacAlister discovered the art of poetry as a healing ritual many years ago. Her poems conjure spell-binding images of intricate inner worlds and the struggles in our contorted society. She tells stories inspired by her work that have been published in various online literary journals and printed anthologies. Whether it is her work in the hospital or fighting the patriarchy: above all these are stories about human connection and the dreams of revolution.

48. THE VISITATION

Tall kissed-out pale fronds of potted ferns
Adorn the entry, their cool shadows dim
Switching the parlor — — death's last living room — —
Where time hesitates and dark furnishings
Project inarguable dignity.

Bookended by brass casket handles, lids
Too heavy to be raised again must sense
My presence, those defiant eyes I closed,
Who parsed my childish alibis, whose last
Wink nicked the priest, who forced death to hold still
Till her eyes sent light leaping into mine.

LINDAANN LOSCHIAVO

Native New Yorker LindaAnn LoSchiavo, recently Poetry SuperHighway's Poet of the Week, is a member of SFPA and The Dramatists Guild. Elgin Award winner "A Route Obscure and Lonely" and "Concupiscent Consumption" are her latest poetry titles. Forthcoming is a paranormal collection of ghost poems, a collaborative horror chapbook, and an Italian-centric book, "Flirting with the Fire Gods," inspired by her Aeolian Island heritage. She has been leading a poetry critique group for two years. Her latest documentary has advanced to "semi-finalist" at The New York Women's Film Fest. https://linktr.ee/LindaAnn.LoSchiavo

49. REMIXING TO COME TOGETHER

We can do a lot with a broken us.
Doorkeepers; those who arrange
theater tickets, screen visitors,
operate elevators/special services,
accept deliveries for the archive

expanding over time.
Once wardens supposedly
obsolete ancestors were
one trillion views of what
connected until we merge
concierges into one charge
at the entrance no longer
the owner's representative.

THOMAS OSATCHOFF

Thomas Osatchoff, together with family, is building a self-sustaining home near a waterfall. Recent work has appeared in Arteidolia, The Concrete Desert Review, The Elevation Review, and elsewhere.

50. SING A LITTLE SONG BIRDIE

Will a bird sing for me?
a sweet melody that I may recognize
As a call of understanding
a desire to know me?

Oh how this sweet, sweet song
replays in the air
Making my heart jump and my feet beat
knowing, I was heard

Sing for me, little bird
and I will join you with a quiet harmony
In recognition and understanding
That there is more to that sound melody
and that singing soul

ATHENA WILKINSON

Athena Wilkinson is a Brooklyn native currently studying as an undergraduate student at Stony Brook University. She doubles in Music and Women's Gender Studies. During her free time, she creates visual art and writes poetry. Many of her works and performances have taken place at the Riverside Church of New York City.

51. STAIRING DOWN

Your dark steps are stained with memories of history.
A single bulb illuminating the ghosts of your past.
Looking down on the footsteps of the forgotten.
The walls screaming in silence with the stories of old.
But in the end is anyone left to hear your cries?
Or will the cries remain a deafening silence?

TONY FLING

Tony Fling is a graphic artist and amateur photographer, Fling is a 1999 graduate of Richland Northeast High School in Columbia, SC and holds Associates Degrees in Liberal Studies and Web Design from Midlands Technical College, a B.A. in Liberal Studies from Limestone College and Masters in Instructional Technology from Fort Hays State University. He has been working with computer graphics and photography for 26 years and is always exploring media, new techniques and methods.

52. INSTINCTUAL

how to talk with the dead
before you speak
still awhile and listen
can you hear the ongoing conversations
between single breath and solitary heartbeat
between birds
amidst the wind
in electric static
what was already said
what needs to be said
in time you speak
yes you say it—dead reckoning
and better respond
before you know it
you are in the ongoing conversation
note the glowing earth
moss and stone
light sea foam
pulses where you belong
before the gloaming

T.M. HUDENBURG

T. M. Hudenburg is a poet who works by the coast and is glad that this poem was able to
grow wings here and dreamt

53. BIG

despite how much older you get
as you grow up from your problems
there is no height which exists for you
to stand tall enough to never see them again

among the clouds find peace
 seek refuge within the clean air
the distance helps and soon
you won't be counting minutes anymore

you will just be breathing big breaths
in new places you could have never planned

REBECCA HOUSTON

Rebecca Houston is a writer and photographer located in Southeastern Minnesota. Her passions include mental health, health literacy, art, and healing. Her work has been featured on Active Minds, Minneapolis Institute of Art, and Camas Magazine.

54. STEREOTYPES

From month to month when men will bleed
and face those torturous pain,
They'll puke, faint, and plead in their need
driving them from sane to insane.
Only then we can talk what equal right is,
What equal responsibility is?
What equal opportunity is?
What actual equality is?

Is my *dupatta* alright?
Is my neckline too deep?
Will the society judge my character?
Will they call me *beep *beep *beep?
Am I not efficient enough at work?
People often utter,
Women can't hold the pressure!
Will depreciation affect my perks?

If a man works overtime,
"Poor soul, such a hardworking fella."
But if a woman works in the same regime,
"Hawww, is she even working?"

Well, there was a time when the very existed society didn't approve
education for women.
Even today, the ideology exists the same that education should be
limited to men.

*"Zyada padh likh k kya karna h
ghar hi toh sambhalna h"*

Nevertheless,
Do you think educated men and educated women live the exact same
life?
When we talk about equality in this decade,

No men can even think of questions, situations, and consequences,
on what women go through in their daily parade.

AMATULZAAHRA SANWARI

Amatulzaahra Sanwari (aka Zaahra) is a soulful writer who shares her feelings through poetry about surroundings, circumstances, love and life in general. She enjoys travelling and exploring the world around to pick up bits and pieces which lets her live an inspired life. She works in Renewables sector as she believes in saving the world for the future generations to see the beauty of the nature.

55. YOU JUST GET OLD

You just get old, 'til you sit and stare
You just get old, and the sky doesn't care
You just get old, and you are set aside
You just get old, and in a dark room you reside
You just get old and wait for decay
You just get old, and lay in dismay
You just get old, as the wrinkles appear
You just get old, and you grimace and fear
You just get old, as all your loved ones die
You just get old, while you sit and ask why
You just get old and you lie and you lie
You just get old, and you cry and you cry
You just get old, 'til you think no more
You just get old, and die in the clothes you last wore

KEN PATTERSON

Ken is a father, a college graduate, a military veteran, and a writer.

He has published two books and three poems.

In addition, Ken has received several literary awards.

56. IN YOUR VESSEL

I live in this self.
My hands touch the walls
of its losses. This self has
pain to pay. I endure.

It's a story, the self's,
that anyone can see in
those sad eyes and broken voice.
Self is fate and I the unwilling will.

I'm a river down the middle
of a river approaching falls.
Each day the same falls.
The self hears me speak,

Lets me do, relies, depends.
I can only hope the past
recedes with your pain
far off, behind us in memory

and I can be alone.

LAWRENCE BRIDGES

Lawrence Bridges' poetry has appeared in The New Yorker, Poetry, and The Tampa Review.
He has published three volumes of poetry: Horses on Drums, Flip Days, and Brownwood
with Red Hen Press.

←————————— **WRITE. FEEL. PUBLISH** —————————→

NEVER GIVE UP ON YOUR DREAMS. IT'S NEVER TOO LATE

If you liked our work, kindly do give us reviews on
Amazon.com/winglessdreamer. It will mean a lot to our editorial team.
You can also tag or follow us on social media platforms:

Instagram: @winglessdreamerlit @ruchi_acharya

Facebook: www.facebook.com/winglessdreamer

Mail us: Editor: editor@winglessdreamer.com

Sales: sales@winglessdreamer.com

Website: www.winglessdreamer.com

You can also support our small publishing community through
donation:

www.paypal.me/Winglessdreamer

WRITE AND WRITE, AND SET YOURSELF FREE.

BOOKS PUBLISHED BY WINGLESS DREAMER

Passionate Penholders   Passionate Penholders II   Art from heart

Daffodils   Father and I   Sunkissed

Tunnel of lost stories   Overcoming Fear   The Rewritten

BOOKS PUBLISHED BY WINGLESS DREAMER

Fruits of our quarantine

Magic of motivational

Diversity

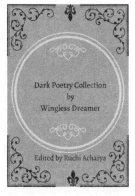

Dark Poetry Collection

A glass of wine with Edgar

Heartfelt

A tribute to Lord Byron

Wicked young writers

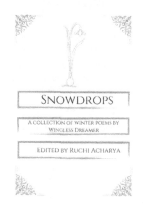

Snowdrops

BOOKS PUBLISHED BY WINGLESS DREAMER

The Wanderlust Within

Writers of tomorrow

BIPOC Issue

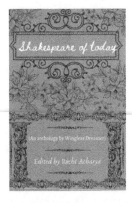

Shakespeare of today

Poem inspired by Robert Frost

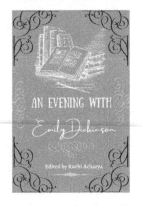

An evening with Emily Dickinson

It's time to snuggle up

Depths of Summer

Flee to Spring

BOOKS PUBLISHED BY WINGLESS DREAMER

How to stay positive

It's twelve o clock

Dreamstones of Summer

Dawn of the day

The book of black

Whispers of Pumpkin

Praised by December

Calling the beginning

Snowflakes and Mistletoes

BOOKS PUBLISHED BY WINGLESS DREAMER

My Cityline

My Glorious Quill

Garden of poets

Let's begin again

Field of black roses

Erotica of eternity

Vanish in Poetry

Oxymorons and Poets

3 Elements Poetry Review

BOOKS PUBLISHED BY WINGLESS DREAMER

Still I rise

Mother, a title just above queen

Ink the Universe

War scars in my heart

The Black Haven

I Have a Dream

Midsummer's Eve

Sea or Seashore

Summer Fireflies